Giver of Life

Confirmation Journal

By Jennifer E. Rooney and Joan Mitchell, CSJ

Good Ground Press

Sisters of St. Joseph of Carondelet
1884 Randolph Avenue
St. Paul, Minnesota 55105

Contents

Photographs: Cleo Photography 4, 12; NASA 9; James L. Shaffer 18
Editorial Development Associates 10, 14, 20, 22, 26, 29, 30, cover.

Nihil Obstat: James M. Lavin
Imprimatur: +Harry J. Flynn, Archbishop of St. Paul-Minneapolis, February 26, 2002.
ISBN 1-885996-12-8

Rights and Responsibilities

Each young person who begins preparing for confirmation must recognize his or her rights and responsibilities as a participant in the program. Your own group may want to add your special concerns to the following rights and responsibilities.

1. **Keep confidential** what others in your group share. Confidentiality is a matter of trust. What any person says in a group stays in the group. Each person's journal is also confidential, off limits to anyone else. Don't look at anyone else's journal without permission, and don't feel you have to let others see what is in your journal. This journal is your own safe place to express yourself.

2. **Listen attentively** to other young people and leaders. Don't be afraid of silence. Please don't interrupt anyone else who is speaking.

3. **Attend all classes.** Participation is key to the process of preparing for confirmation. To participate, you must do more than sit in class. You need to listen, journal, and share your faith.

4. **Take part** in both the enrollment ceremony and the confirmation liturgy. Service is also a requirement of this program.

5. **Respect each other's points of view.** Everyone has the right to his or her opinion. Respect others' feelings and experiences.

6. **Celebrate and play together.** We learn from each other in many different ways. Discussing and faith sharing are important in preparing for confirmation, but taking breaks together and joining in activities will help everyone get to know one another and feel comfortable together.

7. **Don't be afraid to question.** Questioning will help you develop a more adult understanding of Christian beliefs and make your own commitment ultimately stronger.

What Will I Choose?

Ask your parents or a parent to sit down with you and look through your baby book and pictures. Discuss *you* as part of the family. Ask your parents such questions as:

■ What was the day of my birth like?

■ How did my birth affect our family? Brothers, sisters, older, younger? How does my life affect our family now?

■ What do you think is the best thing about being a member of our family?

■ What was my baptism like?

■ What do you think is the best thing about being a member of our parish?

Write a summary of your discussion with your parents or guardians. To get started, use the phrases below.

I am important to my family because _____

_____

_____

_____

_____

My family values our Catholic faith community because _____

_____

_____

_____

_____

The We Plan

If life were an *I* plan, each of us would need only to be concerned about ourselves. It's not. Nearly every activity of life connects each of us to others, which gives us the *we* plan. When we freely make and choose our connections, they are usually more rewarding than those connections we are forced to make. God has given us the freedom to connect and the freedom to choose.

The statements below concern the *we* in your life.
Fill in the blanks with your choices.

1. I love going to the movies with _____.

2. If there is one person I can trust, it's _____.

3. The person I respect most is _____.

4. I have the most fun hanging out with _____.

5. When it comes to my family, _____
is the person I confide in most.

6. I wish I had more time to spend with _____.

7. Every time I hear the song _____,

I immediately think of _____.

8. _____ makes me laugh harder than anyone else.

9. I think _____ would consider me one of his or her best friends.

10. _____ is my favorite hobby, and it's more fun when I

can share it with _____.

Journal

Journal endings to the following two prayers.

Creator God, you surround me with good things and make me free.
I choose to . . .

_____

_____

_____

In this Confirmation Program I want to explore this
about you, God . . .

_____

_____

_____

_____

Faith Sharing
Share your two prayers with your sponsor. Your sponsor will also share with you how he or she finishes these prayers.

Six Days of My Creation

Imagine your life as six days of creation. What events, people, accomplishments, and crises mark definite stages and changes in your becoming the person you are? Who and what has helped create the person you are now?

Identify six of the major causes of change or maturity in your life. These will be the "days" of your creation. Use the spaces below to illustrate your creation. You can write, draw, color.

In the beginning God created the heavens and the earth. The earth was a formless void. Darkness covered the face of the deep. The Spirit of God hovered over the face of the waters.

Genesis 1.1-2

God created humankind in God's image; in God's own image, God created them; male and female God created them.

Genesis 1.27

In the beginning

1

2

3

Enrollment

The confirmation process offers you an opportunity to exercise your freedom to change yourself. You can choose to open yourself up and let the Spirit move in you and through you. At your baptism your parents and godparents agreed to introduce you and guide you in faith. Since then, you have grown in maturity and received the tools necessary for you to make your own free decision to be a committed Christian. Do you want to accept, release, and share your spirit and the Holy Spirit in you?

If you answer yes and want to commit yourself to the process of preparing for confirmation, it only makes sense to share this exciting choice with your faith community. This is what enrollment is about—sharing your openness to the Spirit and affirming your faith. During enrollment you share this intent and your community pledges to support you in this process.

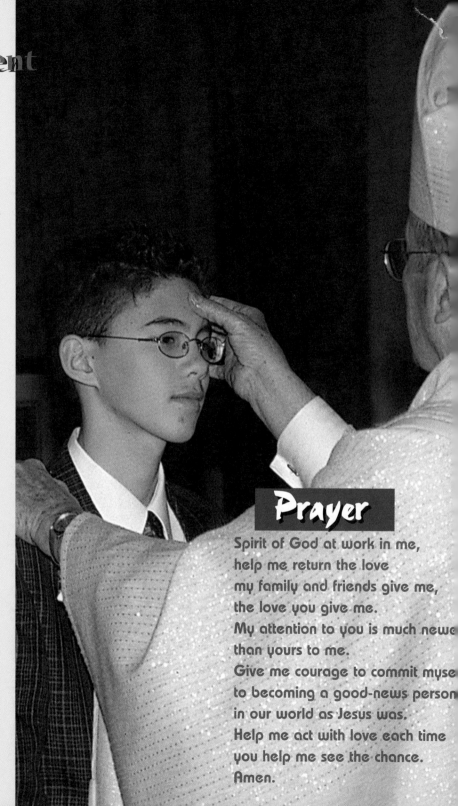

Prayer

Spirit of God at work in me,
help me return the love
my family and friends give me,
the love you give me.
My attention to you is much newe[r]
than yours to me.
Give me courage to commit myse[lf]
to becoming a good-news person
in our world as Jesus was.
Help me act with love each time
you help me see the chance.
Amen.

How Scripture Names the Spirit.

It's very easy to label others. Is it as easy to label ourselves honestly? Use the words at right to fill your name tag with as many words as fit you. Add your own words, too.

Gang Member Smart Cliquey

Skater Shy Carefree Energetic

Wild Ugly

Honest Musical

Youngest

Rich

Hello, I Am....

Thin

Jock

Happy

Violent

Poor

Short Cute Tall

Bookworm Romantic Unmotivated

Male Artistic Funny Ambitious

Pretty Tree Hugger Serious Loving

Handsome

Couch Potato Caring Overweight Loyal

Middle Class Oldest Organized Female

Faith Sharing

The questions below are for you and your sponsor to discuss.

- What makes someone fit the label "good Christian?"

- Can I be a good person if I am not a good Christian? Why or why not?

- Do I have to be Catholic to be a good Christian? Why or why not?

- How does the label "good Christian" fit me?

- What questions do I have about faith? about the Spirit?

- What are my doubts about God?

Journal

We all have moments in our lives where we can feel God's presence. We can feel the Spirit working through us.

Journal about a time when you felt exceptionally close to God or when you could feel the Spirit working through you.

_____

_____

_____

_____

_____

_____

_____

Journal about your favorite bible story or the event in Jesus' life you wish you could have witnessed.

_____

_____

_____

_____

We live in a society that labels to understand. Unfortunately, in our rush to label, we completely discredit or forget many feelings, ideas, and experiences. The same can be said of the seven gifts of the Holy Spirit. The Spirit blesses us with many more gifts than just seven. Take some time and use the prayer to help you recognize the numerous gifts the Spirit brings to your life.

Prayer

Generous Spirit, you give me the tools I need to make right decisions.
You give me the drive to act and the awareness to appreciate your power.
Yours is the energy that draws people together.
Thank you for being there in my loneliness, for opening my eyes to injustice,
for blessing me as a member of a loving faith community.
Add to the prayer.

For this and so much more I offer this prayer.   Amen.

Sensing the Spirit: Spirituality

Faith Sharing

Spirituality is our response as whole persons with bodies, minds, feelings, and relationships to the presence of the Spirit in our lives. Our spirituality expresses our relationship, our communication with God, and our confidence in that relationship. Discuss spirituality with your sponsor, using the questions below to help you.

■ Why do I pray?

■ What do I count on God for?

■ What can God count on me for?

■ When do I pray?

■ How do I pray?

Journal

What does God look like? Draw a picture. How does God feel about me? Write or draw to answer.

Describe your experience of any of the following happenings in your life.

My most awesome experience in nature.

A tragic thing I've experienced.

_____

_____

_____

A discovery I've made about who I really am and what I can do.

_____

_____

_____

A struggle I experienced in a friendship.

_____

_____

_____

A painful experience I've had in my life.

_____

_____

_____

Where Am I With My Spirituality?

We are part of a society that thrives on statistics. We measure, calculate, and pinpoint. Spirituality is not about measuring but about responding to the Spirit within us and around us. So many young people feel discomfort because they don't know where they are spiritually. Is my spirituality level normal for someone my age? Am I on the right track? Do the sacraments I have received mark my spiritual growth?

We can't measure the presence or power of the Spirit in us; we can only realize the Spirit is with us. Recognizing the Spirit works in us urges us in countless, daily, small ways to respond and keep becoming deeper, more spiritual people.

The sacraments of baptism, confirmation, and eucharist initiate us into the life of the Christian community. The Church calls us to join weekly in Sunday eucharist to nourish our spiritual lives and keep becoming more like Jesus. Spirituality grows with time, maturity, and participation in the life of the community.

Our spirituality calls us to question our beliefs and feelings. Only by questioning can we discover what makes our relationship with God special. Acknowledging we have a relationship with God and keeping ourselves open to growth are the most important things any of us can do for our spirituality.

Prayer

Holy Spirit, stir me into action. May your presence become obvious to others in my words and deeds. You dwell within me; I am incomplete without you.
Allow me to be a sign of your love. Amen.

Building Up the Body of Christ: Sacraments

We usually celebrate sacraments in church. That does not mean sacraments happen only inside buildings filled with pews. Sacramental experiences occur frequently in our lives.

When I was a kid, my siblings and I had to pick rocks out of the field during the summer. It wasn't a fun job when the weather was cool, but when it was hot, picking rocks was one of the worst jobs in the world. Your sweat was like a magnet for the dirt that clung to the rocks.

The chatter that filled the air when we started walking the field had usually died down to an occasional mumble by the time we were done. We were exhausted by the time we got home. And then my mom would hook the garden hose up to the sprinkler. Sometimes we'd be too tired to put our swimsuits on and we'd run under the cold water in our dirty work clothes.

No matter how little energy we had when the water first shot into the air, we were always completely refreshed and laughing by the time we were called in to dry off. This was a baptism of sorts—new life-renewed spirit delivered through the sign of water.

Journal

With this story in mind, journal about a sacramental experience that has happened in your daily life. Ask yourself: When have I experienced the renewing effects of water that we celebrate in baptism? When have I experienced the power of sharing food to bond people together? When have I experienced my family remembering relatives I was born too late to know?

Faith Sharin

The questions below are for you and your sponsor to discuss.

■ What do I remember about the celebrations of the sacraments in which I have taken part so far?

■ What are my first memories of going to church?

■ What makes me feel involved in my parish?

■ What do I know about my patron saint?

Ways to Participate in Eucharist

Find out about the following ministries of the Lord's table in your parish. Interview a person who does one of the ministries you think you would most like to do.

- Music ministries
- Playing an instrument
- Singing in the choir
- Handing out music
- Welcoming worshipers
- Taking up the collection
- Serving coffee after Mass
- Driving people to church
- Cleaning the church
- Befriending people who need help getting into the building
- Putting together the church bulletin
- Priest
- Lectors
- Eucharistic ministers
- Servers
- Acolytes
- Ushers

Use the following questions to help you with your interview.

- What is the role of your ministry?
- Who is affected by your work?
- What do you like most about it?
- What gifts or talents do you possess that help you in your ministry?

Prayer

Unceasing Spirit,
you wash away our emptiness
and welcome us into your community.
You forgive our brokenness
and accept us as people
who make mistakes.
You invite us to your table and share
your life with us.

Spirit, you move in us,
guiding us toward you,
through relationships,
through connections and commitment.
You not only drive and impel us,
we find comfort and rest in you as well.
It is by your constant presence
we are made whole. Amen.

Giving Life: Service

To be Catholic Christians, we need to be more than people who participate in Mass on Sunday. We must be people of action, people of service. Responding as a Christian requires the Spirit working in us and with us.

Look at the situations below and write your response. After you've finished, look over them and decide if you're moving in the Spirit.

1. You did poorly on a test . . .

2. Someone punches you . . .

3. Your boy/girl friend is pressuring you to try having sex . . .

4. Your team beats your longtime rivals in the regional tournament . . .

5. Your parents tell you they're getting a divorce . . .

6. Your best friend gets involved in a gang . . .

7. Someone makes fun of you for being Catholic . . .

8. You blow out your knee at ball practice . . .

9. You know your elderly neighbor is sick . . .

10. You know people in your city are homeless . . .

Journal

What evils and wrongs in our world pain me?

The Spirit can work through things that cause us pain to urge us into action for justice.

_____

_____

_____

_____

_____

_____

_____

What experiences of prejudice against me have

I had? Or, what experiences of being treated as an inferior?

_____

_____

_____

_____

_____

_____

_____

What is just and fair? What is unjust and unfair? What do I see as injustices in the world today and what solutions can I think of to make these situations fairer and better?

Faith Sharing

Questions for you and your sponsor to discuss:

■ What service do I enjoy doing most?

■ How do I act as a sign of the Spirit outside of church?

■ To what situation or crisis in the world have I as a Christian felt I had to respond?

Prayer

Spirit of Life,
you blessed and anointed Jesus
who came among us—
a commoner, a teacher, a healer,
a family member, a neighbor,
a miracle worker, a human,
the Father's Son with whom
you live in one love.
Jesus made your love visible
to all who knew him.

Let us keep his story alive
in the way we live.
Let us become a people
of loving actions
who follow the path
Jesus walked for us. Amen.

Sealed in the Spirit: Confirmation

What's in a Name?

Parents introduce us to the Church at baptism when we receive our names. Parents and godparents sponsor us as members of this community. They agree to share their faith with us, to support us in learning about Christian beliefs, and to help us develop a spirituality. Many people have taught, encouraged, and mentored you to reach this moment in your life when you accept responsibility for your own faith and spirituality.

Confirmation completes your initiation into the full life of Christians. At confirmation, you may again take a name or affirm your baptismal name. Your sponsor will accompany you to be sealed with the gift of the Spirit. What is the difference between your baptism and your confirmation? At confirmation, you make the choices. You have already chosen a sponsor. Now you can choose a name or affirm your name.

How do you choose a confirmation name? Choose a name that means something to you. Here are different ideas to help you.

■ Choose the name of a saint who represents a cause you find important.

■ Choose the name of someone in the bible whom you admire.

■ Choose the name of someone in your life who has influenced your faith or has been a living witness of the Spirit to you.

■ Affirm the name your parents gave you at baptism.

When you have chosen your confirmation name, write it below. Do more than just print it. Design your name to illustrate why you have chosen it. For example if you choose the name Isidore, because you know he is the patron saint of farmers and you like to garden, then decorate your name and paper surrounding it with images such as green plants or a hoe.

Journal

How do I think I have grown

in faith through the process of preparing for confirmation? Do I feel I have opened myself to the Spirit? Am I ready for confirmation?

_____

_____

_____

_____

_____

_____

_____

_____

_____

_____

_____

_____

_____

_____

_____

_____

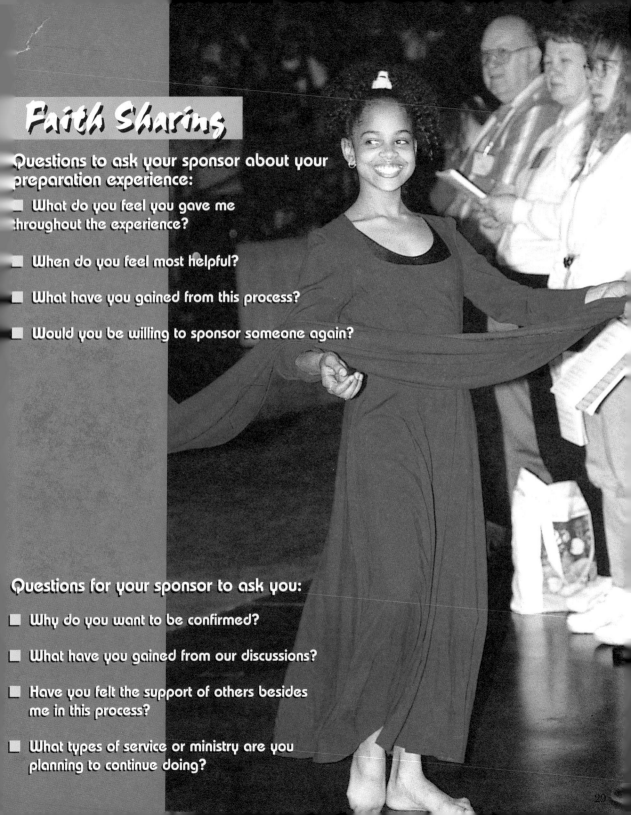

Faith Sharing

Questions to ask your sponsor about your preparation experience:

- What do you feel you gave me throughout the experience?

- When do you feel most helpful?

- What have you gained from this process?

- Would you be willing to sponsor someone again?

Questions for your sponsor to ask you:

- Why do you want to be confirmed?

- What have you gained from our discussions?

- Have you felt the support of others besides me in this process?

- What types of service or ministry are you planning to continue doing?

Prayer

Life-giving Spirit,
I am ready to take
another step
on my journey.
I can barely see the point
from which I started
and I cannot yet see
the place where I may rest,
but I am ready
to take another step.

There have been obstacles,
including myself,
and wrong turns
down one-way streets
where I followed others.
But I am learning to listen
and trust in your word.
I am ready
to take another step.

I am not alone
and must not forget
about the others.
My burden is less
and my benefit greater
when we walk together,
knowing everyone counts.
I am ready
to take another step.
Amen.

Prayer Starters

Use the following statements to help you pray. Your *Confirmation Journal* does not end with session 6 but invites you to make prayer and reflection an ongoing spiritual dimension of your life.

God, I want to tell you what I'm most afraid of...

Where do I see your presence, God?

God, I want to tell you what I'm most proud of...

God, what I am most thankful for is...

God, I feel so discouraged about...

God, in you I find the freedom to . . .

The part of my faith I have the most difficulty accepting. . .

Dear God, my attitude about _____ is not what it should be. Help me. . .

Spirit, I need your gift of . . .

A Big decision is weighing on my mind.
I ask you, God, for the strength and tools necessary for you to make the right decision. What I really need is. . .

Write a litany of the saints in your life. After each person's name, add the words, "Pray for us."

Create a psalm of praise for creation in which each line begins with a new letter of the alphabet in order. For example, you might begin, "Awesome is your world."

Service Evaluation Sheet 1

■ What type of service did I perform?

■ Was it what I expected?

■ What did I like most about this service experience?

■ What did I like least?

■ How did I benefit from this service?

■ Besides myself, who did this service benefit?

■ What did I learn from this experience?

Service Evaluation Sheet 2

■ What type of service did I perform?

■ Was it what I expected?

■ What did I like most about this service experience?

■ What did I like least?

■ How did I benefit from this service?

■ Besides myself, who did this service benefit?

■ What did I learn from this experience?

Service Evaluation Sheet 3

■ What type of service did I perform?

■ Was it what I expected?

■ What did I like most about this service experience?

■ What did I like least?

■ How did I benefit from this service?

■ Besides myself, who did this service benefit?

■ What did I learn from this experience?

Our Father

The *Our Father* is the common prayer of all Christians. Use the questions on this page to reflect on the meaning of this prayer Jesus taught us.

■ **Read Luke 11.1-4 to find out where the *Our Father* comes from and why we say it.**

The first half of the *Our Father* is about God. In this prayer Jesus draws on the experience most people have of loving parents to help us know God loves us as fathers and mothers love their children.

■ **How have I experienced God's love for me?**

God's kingdom is not an earthly kingdom with geographical boundaries but a community of followers from every age and from every nation on earth. Wherever Christians love one another, share what they have, include others, forgive one another, there Jesus reigns. The kingdom of God is a kin*dom, the community of those who believe and live as kin of God.

■ **Where do I see the kin*dom of God coming among us?**

In the second half of the *Our Father* we pray for our own needs—for daily bread, for forgiveness, and for freedom from evil.

■ **What is daily bread? What besides food do people need to survive? To whom in my life do I give daily bread? From whom do I receive daily bread?**

■ **How do I forgive? How do I want to be forgiven?**

■ **What evils do I wish God to protect me from? What can I do about keeping these evils from others?**

Our Baptismal Promises and the Creed of Christians

The promises our parents make for us at baptism summarize the faith of the Christian community. The promises state the same beliefs we proclaim when we pray the *Apostles'* or the *Nicene Creeds*. The bishop will invite candidates to renew their baptismal promises to begin the celebration of the sacrament of confirmation.

Under each of the four baptismal promises below collect your own reflections on the faith it summarizes. During the time you are preparing for confirmation, you may hear sermons and join in discussions that give you insights into the beliefs all Christians profess. Write these insights down here.

Do you believe in God the Father almighty, creator of heaven and earth?

Do you believe in Jesus Christ, his only Son, our Lord, who was born of the Virgin Mary, was crucified, died, and was buried, rose from the dead, and is now seated at the right hand of the Father?

Do you believe in the Holy Spirit, the Lord, the giver of life, who came upon the apostles at Pentecost and today is given to you sacramentally in confirmation?

Do you believe in the holy catholic Church, the communion of saints, the forgiveness of sins, the resurrection of the body, and life everlasting?

God's Word for Your Life

When you need rest and peace, read Matthew 11.28-30.

When you worry, read Matthew 6.25-34.

When you are lonely or fearful, read Psalm 23.

When you need peace of mind, read John 14.27 or Philippians 4.6-8.

When people fail you, read Psalm 27.

When you grow bitter or critical, read 1 Corinthians 13.

When you have done wrong, read Psalm 51 or Luke 15.3-7.

When you are discouraged, read Psalm 34 or Lamentations 3.22-24.

When God seems far away, read Psalm 139.

When the world seems bigger than God, read Psalm 90.

When in sickness, read Psalm 41.

When you feel troubled, read John 14.1-20; Psalm 46.

When in danger, read Psalm 91.

When you want courage, read Joshua 1.1-9.

When you need assurance, read Romans 8.22-39.

When you forget your blessings, read Psalm 103.

When you leave home to travel, read Psalm 121.

When you think of investments, read Mark 10.17-31.

When you need guidelines for living, read Matthew 5 or Romans 12.

When you need to remember the ten commandments, read Exodus 20.1-17.

When you think you will fail, read Isaiah 55.6-13.